EACH LEAF SINGING

EACH LEAF SINGING

poems

Caroline Boutard

MoonPath Press

Copyright © 2021 Caroline Boutard

All rights reserved.

No part of this publication may be reproduced, distributed, or transmitted in any form or by any means whatsoever without written permission from the publisher, except in the case of brief excerpts for critical reviews and articles. All inquiries should be addressed to MoonPath Press.

Poetry
ISBN 978-1-936657-60-5

Cover art by Anthony Boutard, woodcut

Author art by Anthony Boutard, woodcut

Photos by Anthony Boutard

Book design by Tonya Namura, using Minion Pro

MoonPath Press, an imprint of Concrete Wolf Poetry Series, is dedicated to publishing the finest poets
living in the U.S. Pacific Northwest.

MoonPath Press
PO Box 445
Tillamook, OR 97141

MoonPathPress@gmail.com

http://MoonPathPress.com

for Anthony

Table of Contents

Preface	3

i. A Farming Education
Old Oak	7
ATV	8
April Is Cold this Year	10
Cold Comfort	12
A Farming Education	13
Ayers Creek Seasons	14
Haiku: Spring	16
Resources	17
Haiku: Flowering Farm	18
Life of the World to Come, Amen	19

ii. Winter Song for Anthony
The Call	23
Winter Song for Anthony	24
Evening Music	26
Domesticity	28
Nantasket Beach: August 1980	29
Nativity	30
Over the Rainbow	32
Orange	33
Camembert	34
4 Glover Circle, Somerville MA	35

iii. Bird Time
We Came Upon the Body	39
California Quail	41
Bird Time	43
Haiku: Fellow Living Things	45
Payback	46
Starling	47
For the Birds	49

Avian Economics   50
Playing Telephone   52
Haiku: Bird Stories   53
Great Horned   54
Wild   56
Tundra   58
Slow Saints   59

iv. Thinking of You
Thinking of You   63
Farm to Table   64
Bad Love   66
Hard Weather   67
You've heard the one   68
Adytum: April 2020   69
Your Words   71
Some Poems   72
Dog Days   73
Hike   74

v. Sometimes It's So Beautiful Here
Farm   77
Chicory Harvest   79
You, Then I   81
Orchard   83
Garden on Thanksgiving Morning   84
Pruning the Orchard   86
January Lonely   88
Winter Marriage   90
Walk with Me Through the Field   91
He Calls Me from the Road   92
Sometimes It's So Beautiful Here   93

Gratitude and Acknowledgments   95
About the Author   97

EACH LEAF SINGING

Preface

For more than twenty years, my husband and I have led a farming life. In summer, we grow grain and a wide range of beans, vegetables, and fruit. In the fall, we make preserves. During winter, we harvest greens and roots, and grind corn, barley, chick peas and wheat.

Ayers Creek Farm is perched on a wildlife corridor, an east-west passage between the Coast Range and the Tualatin Ridge, as well as on a north-south migratory route. We share our lives and the land with the creatures that travel across our acres.

We named Ayers Creek Farm after the source which feeds its irrigation. This land was once part of the large winter settlement of the Atfalati peoples who lived here for centuries. The Atfalati hunted in the mixed wood forests to the east and gathered Wapato corms for food in the Wapato Lake below, perhaps siting their housing with the same view of the Tualatin valley that we enjoy. While digging in the garden one morning, large pieces of flint and obsidian rolled off my spade. The first people who lived here would have carried the flint from the glacial quarries one hundred miles to the south and traded for the obsidian from the volcanic caldera in the Cascade Range. They might have buried these stones for safe keeping before smallpox and guns drove their community to the reservation sixty miles away. European settlers took over the land, partially draining the lake and planting crops in the Labish muck. The flint and obsidian, the Wapato corms, the flint corn we grow and the land I call home have older stories with other names than what my husband and I know them by.

Anthony will die soon and our life on this land will go with him. We will leave having enjoyed the gift of this time deeply. Ayers Creek Farm has been a third part of our long marriage and given me a steady purchase from which to write. I hope this book reveals my gratitude for all that I have learned working beside Anthony as wife and partner on the soil.

i.
A Farming Education

Old Oak

I leave the work and rush out
to early spring
with no more plan than a good walk
as robins and juncos,
flashing like jackknives,
cleave low angles of afternoon light.
No route than stepping round the mud,
I pass through a veil of smoky air,
its note of orange blossom
from old oak dried slow,
then burned in a clean hearth,
to breathe in
this sweet musk and find
every grassy thing along the way roused
by the warm day, their stems extended
like antennae tuned to the fresh season.
I stop to harvest
from the ruddy mix of plants
galloping through the field—
sow thistle and poppy,
wild radish, dandelion, cress,
so full of healing
you have to eat them standing up,
everything around me
pushing toward renewal.
The plan here is more life,
then more.

ATV

I know the way you picture me
as I manage my farm life of little jobs—
big footed, eyes down,
dragging my tools through the field
in a stooped shuffle
like a mock-up of human
before people became fully upright.

You don't include my ATV
in the sober congregation
of sister trowel and brother hoe—
no muffler, shot ball joints
and up to its rims in mud.

Try to understand
how the sap rises in my chest
when the starlings swarm
as they cover the trees with iridescent smoke,
oak leaves falling like letters,
or the authority of ten thousand plums
ripening in the heat.

Some green fury makes me
press the throttle down and everything
becomes heroic—
fast enough to loosen the tug
of hive and grain
and let all things that can't be fixed
tumble away into the tall grass by the track.

When I come to the line of poplars
marking the end of my land,
I turn around.

Picture me back to work on my knees,
pulling thistles down a long row,
listening to the *tsk, tsk, tsk*
of a two-stroke engine
as it cools in the silence.

April Is Cold this Year

and the garden looks spent.
Dry stalks rise above the duff
like shipwrecked masts,
the ground below humped
and rumpled by frost.

What life there is
lives underground with voles
who crop the meaty fingers of the roots
and line their nests with last year's stubble.

Only the camellias, sporting
their fat gloss, flutter
and adjust themselves in the arctic air.
The chill has leaked into our house,

frosting our exchanges.
We rarely talk these days
as if it's too hard
to push words back and forth

through the underwater gloom
of our kitchen.
Stuck too long indoors, forgetting
how it is to be startled by beauty,

I walk into the woods
for the deep green caramel of mosses
splashed over the logs and theaters of lichen,
their vast cities
hanging from the branches overhead,
lush growth saturating
the rutted hide of the trunks.

Returning, I find you,
your back to the window
with its climbing rose you say

is over-crowding its neighbors.
Never joining me outside,
you've stayed close to the house these days,
warming yourself
in the glow from your laptop.

But I have the orbit of the earth on my side—
May will open her palm,
fragrance fattening the air,
soon I will prop the backdoor open to the sun
while you stand up to hunt for your pruners.

We will walk outside,
our conversation gentled
by the soft boom of open air,
and I will agree with you
about the rose and everything else.

Cold Comfort

Just day-break and already tired
from pushing the world uphill,
I slam out of our house
to a cold November farm.

Past work waiting,
work unlikely to get done,
I walk, abandoning the promises I made
to us, to the farm as well.

Bruised by my boots,
the rich musk of Queen Anne's lace
rises around me in the meadow—
sharp and astonishing.

Geese slide over the treetops,
aiming toward the wetlands,
their bodies blending
with the whites and greys below.

I join the flock, wings
breaking through flesh
as the world rights itself.

I tuck it all close, this fat purse—
the good and the bad clinking.

A Farming Education

Planting potatoes in the early spring soil,
I practice the arc of my own reach and balance,
the strength I can count on to lift the pail,
the right measure of a pace
as I bend, step, bend along a five-hundred-foot row,
placing each soft, tan soul right-side up.

Awkward in city rooms now,
clothes not feeling right,
I sit carefully on the edge of the chair,
reach for my cup with rough hands
and talk about city things,
trying to remember the trick of it.

People ask with a hopeful tone,
my kind friends who worry,
what sort of work we are doing these days
and if we miss our city life—
I think *potatoes*
and the memory rings in my chest like a bell.

Ayers Creek Seasons

      i.
Our barn stands, shining—
the Ark atop a new world's
first dry hill.

Soil trampled by months of rain,
but everywhere fresh green
points toward light.

Breeze lays a warm hand against my back
as I kneel to plant seedlings,
tucking each into the loamy row.

      ii.
This plump time of summer
noisy with enterprise!
I shout and the earth opens.

Manna falls from the stalk.
I pretend there is plenty
for the whole world.

The sun stalks mid-day.
We cower in shadow
from this mighty beast.

      iii.
Fall bends me to the ground.
as I harvest green life
that flickers around me in the mist.

We wait for our own harvesting
as time swings her dark bell,
marking our toll.

A heron lifts
her wings in benediction,
dissolving back into the fog.

      iv.
The corn stalks wave tattered standards
in a winter storm. Below,
quail glean scattered grain.

Short days drowse into night
as percussions of rain
drum against my sleep.

In my dream, November rolls
Jupiter and Mars toward the horizon,
crushing our tiny span
fine as last summer's leaves.

Haiku: Spring

Soon the bees return.
My table is still sticky
from last year's honey.

We watch the corn plants
leaf out in long, even rows—
weeds will fill each gap.

Pruning the orchard
as the spring rain wets the crowns—
shining branches fall.

Robin eggs have hatched,
but become tasty morsels—
crows must feed their young.

Time for ripening—
the cherries are small green balls.
The birds still pick them!

Resources

The winter rain begins slowly,
then builds to a steady sigh
on the roof above my head.
It falls into the lake,
spilling ducks over the dike.
It fills up green cups of cabbages
left in the field,
shattered by winter.
Rain rides down to the gutters
and onto the ground.
It runs over the edge of the bucket by the door,
spattering onto the mat, hard beads animating
specks of soil and moss—
not a drop wasted if it makes a poem.

Haiku: Flowering Farm

Flat soups in springtime—
last year's beans and few fresh greens.
Time to plant more seed.

The hellebore blooms
in the worst of the weather—
a plant worth growing.

Mustard is chromic:
in the field, bright yellow;
on hot dogs, mustard.

Too much April rain.
All pollination has ceased—
no fruit this summer.

Some flowers smell bad.
Some have thorns and toxic sap—
bees don't give a damn.

Life of the World to Come, Amen

Another harvest ruined as pollen explodes
down twenty rows of beans,
all wilting in the heat—
water turned to sewage
from our neighbor's run-off waste—
spring too early and winter too rough—
smoke choking the night.

The Earth sighs
and cannot reach her wounds.
I watch our world
phosphoresce
in the smog above
my head.

In my dreams
I am a weary supplicant
in the long line
at nightclub Heaven—
winged bouncer at the door,
my request for absolution denied.

Every morning,
relieved to find the garden still full of beauty
as silly and precious as a
favorite plastic toy,
I pick up my life and march, waving.

ii.

Winter Song for Anthony

The Call

You deliver the news
as if our disaster
were an ordinary trouble,
noises behind you in the hospital
sound like skirmishes of war.
Our garden was trampled
by frost in the night—
unrecognizable, flattened
like someone,
let's call them an innocent victim,
struck by a bullet, sprawled awkwardly
on the ground,
like you, caught just so
by a diagnosis.
You, also innocent,
also mortified by terrible luck.

Winter Song for Anthony

We watch the sparrows fill themselves
with grain you have spread in the rain—
birds give you so much pleasure,
their squabbles, their eager rushing.

As we stand, staring toward the west,
my eye moves through leafless tangle
past the meadow to hills dusty with snow.

Here I am in the foreground,
blocking the view
to find a place for me in this poem
about you on your way downhill.

Illness is a burden you have shouldered for a while.
You do this well, mostly alone.
I help, the way I did
when we brought our first couch up the stairs
and I barely carried the weight of my share.

Already, you are giving away your extra cargo—

>   the car you love to fix
>   coins from your grandfather
>   your favorite jazz.

You lost your faith long ago in a god
who could save us now,
but kept your affection for the holiness
of church music,

>   the long chords of Mozart's
>   *Great Mass in C* ascending toward
>   the vault of some German cathedral,

Hosanna floating up
to the oak and stone.

Along the ridgeline, the bare trees
seem to rise in the air,
lighter without their leaves.
You, also rising,
letting me go for more lift.

Evening Music

On the long kitchen nights
of our winters,
music becomes the conversation.
Settled after the meal,
we shed what we can of the day
as opera presses up against our burdens,
like the wet nose of a large dog
who loves you and wants your attention.

Sometimes,
Hermann Prey does the heavy lifting
with something he sings so well
from the Marriage of Figaro,
each verse a bite-sized confection,
sweetening the evening.

After so much was lost to fire,
grief needed a sound track—
Lorraine Hunt Lieberson, dying of cancer,
healed us with Bach's 82nd—
it is enough, it is enough,
spaces of silence in the descant
as vast and cleansing
as the deep knell of her voice.

When you are lifted up
by a good score,
a high window opens—
not to your own life, but to somewhere
shared by everyone who ever heard
music as fine
as the glad hymn of
Count Basie's blues,
the swing bringing

its big kisses and hugs
but really talking about the promised land,
or the heartbreak
of Bill Evans' *Piece for Peace*—
his head close to the keyboard,
concentrating on the black and white
like a master carpenter
building his own coffin.

Domesticity

Running out with you to rescue laundry
as a storm rushes in from the south—
how the sheets flap, calling us!
Charged, humming with soap and lavender,
horizons of linen snap with gusts
that rise up

toward a thin broth of clouds scattering.
We hug handfuls of cloth that roll around us,
jamming clothespins in every pocket,
then a slap of thunder
then and
then

and the tailing off now
as fat drops explode on the flagstones
till the storm gentles to a steady release
of water falling.

Side by side on the porch,
we watch how everything opens to the wet.
Close beside you,
your warmth dries the rain on my skin—
our animal bodies talking.

Nantasket Beach: August 1980

As if we two were born out of sea,
we returned every chance to this shore
to run over the sand,
and throw ourselves
toward horizon's vast mouth.

Rushing through the waves,
there was nothing else that summer
but to drift in the salt. Two rafts—
only our souls aboard.

Conversation losing its importance
with the rough pleasure of motion,
we floated free, moving our arms
to keep our breath above
the ocean's great machinery.

Bathed with a light against which
everything inland dimmed
my body glowed under the wet,
its fabric breaking up,
then re-making in the swells.

So much of that fullness
we carried back to shore.
Once empty, we returned for more.

Nativity
  for Caroline

The night I gave birth to you
a wind rose up and everything raged.
Something primal kicked neurons awake

to begin the first work. Signals were sent,
hallways and corridors prepared.
Trees knocked against the house
as if they wanted in
and you,
all you wanted was out.
The night—

or was it day? Impossible to know inside
that vault of a hospital ward
with nothing to cover you and me
but a single sheet,

another sheet on a rod between us
and the fifteen-year-old bellowing
in the next stall.
I could not go to help.
We were both
deep in our own temples,
each calling to our own gods.
Scoured smooth
by the pressure of a vast continent shifting,
I groaned in some ancient language
I did not know to speak.

You floated out on a hot inland sea
and I was washed up on the shore
of an unknown territory

and you—
pristine, fragrant, angry for breast,
became my new home.

Over the Rainbow
for my father

I wanted to sing "Over the Rainbow" to you,
dying that afternoon
but you had become an empty house,
your eyes dark windows,
your slack jaw the door open
when everything of value
has already been taken—
your sanctuary trespassed by a rental bed
as strangers managed your body, unconcerned
that summer was burning your garden down.

I wanted to tell you
I remembered our unpredictable dinners,
when the only thing relaxed
was the duck on its platter,
or the time I caught you with my quick joke
and made you laugh—
I loved you so for that.

I wanted to hold your face between my palms,
press life back into your eyes,
and hear you tell me again, again
how much you hated that song.

Orange

Early morning and my grandson
is asking to peel an orange,
rolling want in his bud of a mouth
in juicy anticipation.

He cleaves segment from segment,
breaking the skin
and the air sparks with bright spice,

suspended in this scent
we rest between ticks of the clock.
He leans near
his palm floats toward me holding fruit.

Camembert

Do this for me—
open that ghost town of a fridge
and find the wheel you bought
for the party that didn't happen.
It's still there, wrapped in its gaudy box.
Knowing you, it's not artisanal,
just flash from the market
as you thought no one would care,
celebrating, as we would have been,
with a big win.
So, take off the foil and let it warm.
It won't smell too strong.
It isn't good enough.
This is no gem from a Normandy cave,
fragrant with raw milk and forest.
Peel off the top and throw it
in the compost for your neighbor's cat.
She may forget the sparrows
who sun themselves against the house.
While you're dumping the bucket,
stop by the thyme you planted last spring,
now a wild nest of tiny leaves.
Cut a palm-full of sprigs.
What you don't use today
will remind you that green things endure.
Chop up the leaves and sauté with bacon.
Your house smells better already.
Add garlic and onion
and stretch out your back while everything
relaxes in the heat.
Pour it all on the cheese and put it in the oven.
Then, wash your face and wait for me—
I'll bring the baguette.

4 Glover Circle, Somerville MA
for Denise Levertov and her poem
"The Métier of Blossoming"

Her house sat on a grimy little lane,
overcast by a city on the rise,
front yard empty
except for a trumpet vine
riding the hurricane fence,
its branches exploding out
toward the narrow band of sky,
red flowers waving to passing traffic.

She welcomed me in,
included the vine in her gladness,
then took me through richly colored rooms
filled with books and icons to the back.
I was there to help her make a garden.

A lone patch of ground
sparkled with metallic debris—
small, crushed things breaking the surface.
To one side, Norway maples
made a brave line of bone-dry shade
where nothing I knew could live.
These problems didn't seem to bother her
at all that May.

She imagined lilies and allium, begonias
and campanula growing here
and talked me into seeing them too—
a stubborn grace,
a dark urgency taking hold.

From her verse,
I should have expected

this singular focus she levelled
on living things,
always scouting for
God's thumbprint—
her longing
to "blossom out of herself"
as fine as any amaryllis—
her art declaring
even here,
there is beauty we build toward
that makes it right.
A heart broken by the world,
and still in love with its possibilities,
is entirely reasonable.

iii.
Bird Time

We Came Upon the Body
for Linda

We came upon the body
not understanding until the last
what we were stopped by—
the fresh death of a yearling doe
splayed across our path.

Here we stood, startled to a halt
by the majesty of this terminus
to the ramble we had planned along the dike,
having walked through any number
of swallows as they slid between
fields and woodland,

then down to the wetland,
with its cloud of red-winged blackbirds
clacking their disapproval at our trespass,
past a pair of egrets, and one great blue heron
knee-deep in the creek.

The hunter among us guessed
a cougar had dragged the carcass here—
its snapped spine and broken neck,
the chiseled divide of muscle and meat—
this was death delivered by a mighty jaw.

Abdomen sculpted out in one clean swipe,
heart, lungs, spleen and liver all consumed,
a grey coil of intestines
discarded a few feet away.
The cavity glistened a silky scarlet,
ribs lined up like organ pipes.
There was no blood.
The fine browns of her coat

sprinkled with beads from last night's shower,
her delicate head settled on the turf,
eyes half hooded—
she had moved beyond her terror
when she was culled
from her matriarch's herd.

No smell,
just the clean fragrance of resin
from the poplar grove nearby
and background notes of pollen
floating off the mustard up the slope.

Her haunches still intact,
made my friend the chef think, prosciutto,
but this body was already spoken for—
its owner no doubt waiting for us to leave.

We returned the next day,
expecting to find a grey buzz
working her remains
but she was gone—
the yarrow, plantain, and native fescue
barely mussed.

I remembered her body laid out long,
hind quarters gathered for a big leap
into the next world.

California Quail

Here the quail come now—
their bodies a downy cave
with modest feathering—
the browns and greys of a fall meadow,
their soft chuffing
and plump, upright carriage.

They will not spot you
standing on the porch—
not like the red-tail hawk,
with its battle plumage
which descends like a fist
into the gentle decorum of the garden
to terrify the hummingbirds and doves.

The deacon guides the congregation,
his plume nodding as he walks,
a built-on reminder
to attend to nothing further afield
than safe passage and a small day.

My father called them *game*—
my father, a *pukka sahib*
posing after the shoot,
his fist around his shotgun,
a row of their corpses lined up in front.

Stay long enough
to witness these saints passing by
as they hunt for seed and insects in the grass,
with no destination beyond
the abundance of companionship.

Come back in the house
when you feel the craving
to capture one
and trap its trembling heart
next to your cheek.

Bird Time

Suddenly
the day split in two
when a bird's skull hit the glass.

Spooked by a Cooper's hawk,
an acorn woodpecker
now shivered below my window
in the grass.
Of all its kind, the last I expected
to find there, its eyes half-shuttered,
wings flung wide in something like
surrender to the afterlife.

Such wary birds—
I see them glitter in the twilight of the trees
with their bright feathering,
their two-note caws scissoring the air
as they patrol the boundary
of their woods.

They never dip within
the comforts of the yard,
unlike the quail
who lounge in the garden,
waiting for snacks.

I lift its body,
meaning to bring it to the edge of the trees
and let it fade into the rough privacy there.
Instead, it carries us both
into the wild.

Everything becomes *bird*—
the air crystalizing into flight lines,

applied mechanics of lift and air flow,
of thrust and drag.

All around us
robins plunge deep into manzanitas,
tugging at clusters of brown fruit,
while finches hug wooly stalks of mullein
to pry out seed.

A hummingbird stands in the air,
moving to each tube of salvia floret
in some gentle sacrament.

Ferried between my palms,
the woodpecker floats in half-life
till some inner shore is reached.
After a pause for assessment
and one indignant glare,
it explodes into flight,
straight to the top of the oaks.

Haiku: Fellow Living Things

Gophers feed their young
on my tiny spring lettuce—
why not eat the weeds?

Coleoptera—
my bathroom is now refuge
for one small beetle.

May mornings are cold.
The mice, now fat on spring grain
still huddle for warmth.

Coyotes gather
in the field to howl at night.
Our sleep is over.

I sowed some lettuce
but a rabbit found the plants.
Sharing greens is hard.

Payback

A man's house is burning across the valley,
its domestic rectangle fraying
the line of big leaf maples along the water
as black quakes of smoke
roil up toward the haze,
forming a vertical slash against the hills.

I imagine I can hear
the collapse of the second floor,
furniture exploding, the pop of glass.
As fire drags the house out of square,
geese lift from the lake,
shape slow cursives in the air
then land again.

Last week, the flock flew up,
propelled by the blasts from a gun
of the man who owns that house.
Three dead geese dropped back to the water.

I stay to watch till the smog starts to fade.
The surviving geese forage the bank,
settle again for the night,
ash from the blaze bringing an early twilight.

Starling

All summer,
our neighbors had raged against the birds
for mobbing their land,
vandalizing crops,
and spraying graffiti in swaths
across their barns.
Nests were burned,
feed poisoned,
the sky sprayed with shot.

That day might have been forgotten,
tied to a string of other days,
except for the starling
which appeared as I walked to my work.

Late afternoon sun had cut down
the line of oaks,
their ghosts felled across the road.
Focused on hieroglyphs of light and shade,
I was surprised
by the clear and perfect din of a firetruck
clanging ten feet above my head.

Here was one—
iridescent against the branch—
a showy, clever bird
who cocked her hard eye
and made the sound a second time,
that perfect two-note warning.

The bird and I both turned
to scan the roofline of the house
for any dark smudge rising.

I might have forgotten,
were it not that starlings glean our farm,
rising around us when we pass,
their bodies blazing like fire itself.

For the Birds

Here's the thing—
all my years
I have followed birds
as they tossed out their green hymns
in the branches above my head.
Stranded below,
in my fork and knife life,
I have watched them swim the great blue,
convinced that all that avian clatter
is the gentle knock
of this world's machinery
calling God back to us.
You tell me their songs
are nothing more than big talk
about sex and territory.
So, what should I say—
"Show me what you got, blue jay?"

Avian Economics
for Tina

A western meadowlark arrived
on this warm spring afternoon,
its call notes
rising up
along our pasture fence.

We pause to attend to
a recalibration of the day—
to such sweet portion
of flute and warble,
the mind opening
again and again to the field
as continents of cloud smooth its surface.

This citizen of prairie travelled
from the south,
tracking the dwindling portion
of wild countryside.
The grassland along the ancient route
is plundered early now for hay,
the spray of toxin laid down as prescribed,
as the laws of productive tillage
have advised.

The Sioux valued
their meadowlarks as omens
of friendship and loyalty,
avoiding the shallow dips in grass
that cradle a nest.

The Blackfoot thought them
carriers of peace—

protection of this shy, tawny settler
deemed sound tribal worth.

I take the long way home,
over the past of the Atfalati people
who once lived in this land
and took their own care
for this little traveler
who must find our rough meadow
of grass and herbs well managed
since it seems not managed at all—
a waste of good field
in one neighbor's estimation.

Breezes blade the meadow,
billowing the fescue with its modest flowers,
stroking the clover
and old cornstalks to shake.
Sorrel and chickweed
wave their fat waddings at the margins,
green vapor rising in the eddies.

The meadowlark's stout body
explores the oat and vetch,
its beak prying open the earth
for last summer's grain
and this year's crop of beetle and grub.

Its song follows me,
bright flanks brushing the soft gatherings
of the afternoon—
an answering call rises from the thicket
and always the sky grows larger.

Playing Telephone

My husband hangs up,
turns to me,
says
our daughter
just told our grandchildren
about sin,
and they thought it was hilarious.

Imagine me
imagining the pair of them—
carjacking,
money laundering,
their little heads together,
merrily working their way
through every one
of the seven deadly.

Then, I realize
he'd said Sid,
the family parrot
that had terrorized us all
for years,

and somewhere
in the verdant jungles of heaven,
Sid thinks this is hilarious.

Haiku: Bird Stories

Hummingbirds are mean—
they strafe me at their feeder.
Who will feed them now?

The sprinkler is on.
Cedar waxwings take a bath—
birds and herbs refreshed.

Meadowlarks are back—
their call notes move through the farm.
We stop to listen.

Doves in the driveway—
they stand right in the middle.
At least chickens cross.

Wood ducks lay their eggs
forty feet above the ground—
a test for their young.

Great Horned

Camouflaged in a snag of fir
high above my head,
she turns her glare toward me—
tufted ears, brindled brown-grey feathers
blending smoothly into the tree,
except for the golden iris of her moon eyes.

She and her mate call to one another,
back and forth,
with an urgency that marks
their time to mate as now,
this low-pitched question
only bodies can answer.

Once settled, she presses herself low
through rain and snow,
until one warm day when she stands
to stretch her legs and preen,
three white faces peer into the sunshine.

For ten springs, the pair
have raised chicks in this tree,
starting each brood when the world
is still winter,
enduring my presence,
just as she does all her hardships,
our constant attentions
and daily household clatter
just yards from her nest.

She glides out at sunset—
I would fly away too,
lifting far above my life,
so high the fields become

someone else's unwashed quilt,
not this muddy slog,
tripping over my shovel
as we harvest another long row.
But something about you and I
always calls me back to land.

She is on her nest tonight
and I am below under the same rain,
listening to a dog bark across the valley,
cars slowing down
and making the turn up the hill,
both of us getting on with things,
making it all enough.

Wild

On long afternoons of summer,
coyotes convene in our fields
or the canyon of fir and oak.

A single ululation starts the pack,
then their thick yearnings
are poured into howls.

A choir rises up above
the dull hum on the valley floor
and everything is changed.

They want nothing of us,
the day ghosts
with our dark museum of farm sheds,
our machines that shred the earth,
confusing fragrant tracks of mouse and vole.

They make their own avenues
through the valley's grid of planted rows
and property lines,
the grass marked flat by their passage.

Like us, they love the orchard,
the little Mirabelle plums
and Imperial Epineuse,
the dark Hungarian cherries
so heavy with juice.
All summer, coyote scat is filled with pits.
Only once, a tiny bitch was sick enough
to limp down our driveway

and drag herself beneath the truck.
Panting, she stared into my eyes
until the bullet hit her skull.

Our neighbor asked to hang the corpse
on his fence,
the man who holds a collar
or a pistol behind his back
for all outsiders.

We planted her little body among the plums,
tucked her head in her paws
and curled her up
to sleep under the loam.
Coyotes roam through the garden tonight,
their yips flashing in the dark,
shaking something loose in me
that yips back.
I want them to hear
the woman who tips over trash cans,
rummages through other people's ideas,
takes what she wants,
sniffs out small scraps of truth
from the dust.

Tundra

This morning a swan
dropped dark from the sky,
turning white against the green line of firs
as it spiraled lower,
wing tips curling under to cup the air,
then fluttered to a stop to lower onto the wet.

My husband's better eyes spotted
the black and yellow markings on its bill—
a tundra swan, late for the spring migration
that had passed through weeks before.
We both agreed it must be our bird, returned.

This swan spent two years here,
never once leaving
our six-acre portion of wetland,
floating solo through a mosaic
of tule grass and cattail,
harvesting green weeds
from the rich Labish muck.

Then one day, it lifted off
paired with another of its tribe.
Back a year later and alone,
I worry why,
as if the vantage of our farm
overlooking the lake
gives me some purchase over this swan's fate.

On the ridge at sunset,
I search for that bright speck
tucked somewhere in the water below
as the lines and angles of the fields dissolve
in the gravity of dusk.

Slow Saints

First light glints
through the oaks from the east.
Then, a new sound—
cows
brought here early this morning
by one of the Dyke brothers
to our overgrown chestnut orchard
for summer pasture.

After breakfast, I walk out to see them—
young heifers,
bunched at the corner,
the ground already churned brown
by their hooves.

The herd backs up as I approach,
and nodding with each step,
they turn their faces away
to trudge over this new terrain—
soft pad ears held low,
flanks fluttering off flies,
their tails slap one side, then the other
with the cadence of a scourge,
as if sin is possible
for these little sisters of perpetual nurture.

Unsettled by the clamor of our tragedies,
it's no wonder some pay money to hug cows,
to recline in a meadow with that heavy head
resting on their laps—

maybe no less a burden for a heifer
than the gloved fist
with its semen-filled syringe

pushing them into motherhood.
Then, the long servitude of birthing,
year after year—
most calves taken so young,
milk not yet wet their chins.

I return in the evening
to watch these slow saints gather,
the round arc of their sides
gently nudging the others
as they move together
toward a grove of poplars for the night,
trailing steamy ribbons behind them
of field greens and flowers—
the summer night fragrant with sanctuary.

iv.
Thinking of You

Thinking of You

Crow rises up,
legs trailing,
all muscle spent
on the forward stroke.

Something in my nature
rises up with it,
though somewhere
mid-air
we drift apart.

Crow's design
is for the up-ahead,
while I,
captivated by the downward arc,
circle above you
looking for a place to land.

Farm to Table

The kitchen is open
and the chef is mad.
Reservations were at six
and this farmer is late—
too late now
to wash all the grit off my nails,
I sit where I'm told
and watch the action
as this artisan
lifts his knife.
Beneath his hands,
blade leans into the pulp,
then the *shink* and *bop*
as flesh and leaf swim
in the *yes, yes, yes* of the chop.

The harvest I delivered just this morning
unrecognizable now—
transformed
to high-rise towers
trembling on their plates—
all this pomp, plus tables like bright altars,
the din of easy laughter,
dimly lit glass.

Dinner arrives
and hunger opens me—
I'm focused by want,
absorbed by ribbons of fragrant steam rising.
In the dark house
of my mouth, fantastic creatures couple.
Birds fly down my throat

to roost beneath the ribs
as fish stare up from the dish
hypnotized by my fork.

With each mouthful,
I crush summer between my teeth.

Bad Love

It's my mouth
that's like a dog's—
all slack and simple,
careless words slavering my chin
like spit.
Too loud in public,
nipping hard
when you think it's play.

It's my heart as well—
too friendly to strangers,
an appetite for garbage,
barely faithful,
pulling at this chain
that holds us both.

I must obey.
Make me sit.
Make me stay.

Hard Weather

On my usual route
through the tedium of the city,
I was stopped
by the face of a man
sprinting up the sidewalk,

his shoes tapping on the pavement
ahead of the morning commuters
who moved like sleepwalkers behind him,
their cold-brew and briefcases in hand.

Eyes radiant,
focused on some future point,
he tacked wide, side to side,
beating against some hard weather
of his alone.

He owned the street—
moving so sure, already stretching out
for the snap of a finish line
against his thin chest.

The crutches clipped to his arms
swung like silver oars,
rowing him through the muggy August air.

You've heard the one

about the dying man,
who hauled himself out of bed
to follow the scent of just-baked cookies
only to learn they were reserved
for his funeral?
My mother, dying,
had loved that joke,
and would have laughed again
if her lungs hadn't already turned to stone.
Aside from the humor,
this man's wife had enough mean
to earn my mother's respect.
There were to be no parting hugs—
the stickiness of affection
had always annoyed.
Tears bored her—
if there was wit, you had her attention.
Any weakness was sport, including her own,
complaining when her sister died
that she was left short
of a fourth for bridge.
Her biggest regret was missing spring.
In some heroic gesture,
I brought her an orchard
of plum and cherry branches
which burst into bloom around her bed.
Her old allergy to any pollen
nearly killed her that night.
Gasping through rented oxygen,
she saw the joke.
I couldn't laugh about it when she died.

Adytum: April 2020

As I listen to the news change the world,
sparrows stir the gravel for grain
scattered in the garden before dawn.

Last week, I would have had time
for metaphors—
imagined dawn
shaking the garden free of the night,
seen every iris blade fixed in position,
poised for a *grand allegro*.

No longer—
starting now, everything is literal.

The plants are real, but this talk of dance
has to go, along with exaggerated make-up
and theatrical gestures,
even poetic allusions to dawn are wrong—
the sun does not consider
you or me in its rotation.

The birds can stay.
They live in the real
where a scrub jay jabs its sharp beak
into the robin's nest
and plucks out hatchlings for lunch.

The habit of lunch goes too—
I eat all day, to settle something
sobbing in my gut that has nothing to do
with a sandwich.

This new reality is no vacation,
now that all vacations are out—

like a tourist in my own back yard,
I know less about survival
than the voles who eat my bulbs.

There is nowhere else to go but deep
where my little animal heart flutters,
waiting for something huge
to poke its appetite into my garden,
curious to see if I taste like home.

Your Words

were the best
piece of fruit—
the peach I remember
from summer
still warm
from the orchard
and my mouth fills with
spit and longing—
that gasp between bite and taste,
the sweet and perfect tang,
the taste of being forgiven.

Some Poems

hang back
beyond the firelight.
I follow their yips
as they circle in the dark.

These are skittering, wild things
all lambent muscle and jaw,
coats sparking with voltage.
My fists clutch empty paper—
nothing I have
can coax them close.

They lope ahead
as I follow, confused
by the churn of their tracks—
stumbling headfirst,
the words I hunt
slide south off the page.

At the end of another dry day
at my desk, just as I stop—
a bright tongue licks my hand.

Dog Days

Lucky this morning, I caught
the instant the firs in the canyon
were splashed with first light—
their huge bodies leaning towards each other
like old gods conferring.
Birds, ignited by the sun,
tumbled like gems from their crowns.

By noon, all the great ideas had gone
and the point of it all had wilted in the heat.
I wanted nothing more than to turn the page
and find something glittering in the next day.

Our old dog, braced against my knee,
panting in his ragged coat,
smiled up through cloudy eyes to argue
that every hour held enough pleasure
for both of us.

Let me show you, he said.
So, we sat together on the grass
as he steered the easy afternoon,
while everything restless raced by
on the one-way road toward night.

Hike

Dropping down into the canyon,
heels hard against mountain scree,
we descend past aspens,
their leaves shivering,
the sky cupped between the peaks above.

We walk, not together—
I follow where you decide.
A wary traveler,
top-heavy with my comforts,
I scrabble, head down
over foreign ground.

This world has been scoured
by centuries of disasters moving downhill.
Dizzy from the unfamiliar,
I gasp for air and look behind me.

When we settle,
the distance between us still unmapped,
I stretch my hands out to you from my life
and you move close,
our bodies a compass pointing toward home.

v.

Sometimes It's So Beautiful Here

Farm

We fell in love
with what we had just bought—
a farm two brothers-in-law
had grown to hate, so sold to us.

What we got was plastic rubble
scattered through the rows,
butter tubs and grocery bags
sprouting in the rain,

and oaks felled across roadways,
platoons of cedars drowning in mud,
bottles clogging one shed,
another filled with toxins
and broken toys.

Freed of our bonsai life in a city lot,
we thrived in fresh ground,
embarrassed by our pleasure
like honeymooners caught in bed.

We earned new muscle opening land,
hauled out tons of junk,
scored our palms on wire
rusting under weeds,
then rooted out the weeds as well.

We rescued a hill from a busted bus,
gravid with mattresses and left to rot,
the ground around it glittering with glass,
now covered with manzanita
and native grass.

It took two decades to fix the soil,
crushed to dead pan from hard abuse.

Healing our land, and the patience it took,
was the hardest thing we ever did.

So many things we couldn't mend—
the pumps you broke, the tools I lost,
the covenant we couldn't keep—
to stay here on this farm for life.

Now, the teasel has returned,
along with brambles we thought removed,
the roofs with holes,
and scrap we meant to clear—
so much undone, so much we meant to do.

The next young couple will have to start fresh,
without the former owners' help
to mend the roofs and throw away the trash
and pull the weeds and organize the sheds.

I imagine I'll always feel the twinge
from obligation to this farm,
an ache from years of work in fields
that no longer will be ours to tend.

I watch this morning's bank of mist
the orchard holds above its crowns
and wonder when the weight of all that air
is too much for the oldest trees to bear.

Chicory Harvest

The trick is
to find the center
within the plump furl of outer leaves,
grip the head
and drive the knife deep.

Free the tight heart,
then peel away
all ragged excess of grit and slime
till you hold a spotless core.
Now, do it again. Again.

Clumsy at first,
you soon swing easy into harvest,
your body remembering
an ancient drive to gather crops,
ancestors cradled in your marrow
warmed awake by the work.

As the afternoon ignites
the neighbors' field to gold,
see your shadow reach its hand
across the tarmac
to run itself through the stems of fescue
edging the road—
your double at ease in the meadow world.

Rising up from the stew of mud,
decay rings its musty bell
to announce life passing,
your own breath
adding its animal tang to the great mix.

Above you, one thousand geese
hurry east toward the Cascade Range,

the urgency of their calls astounding,
resounding against
the downslope of the day.

Tonight, in sleep you consider
how it ached to put your back
behind the blade,
the heft of the bucket
you dragged behind you,
how your boots snagged in chickweed—
each step closer to an answer about yourself.

You, Then I

Back from our visit to the doctor,
always together
now that we have
only one life between us,
now that yours
is almost gone.

The glutton
hiding in your bones
is growing into something mighty,
embracing your spine in a feathered spiral,
curling through your hips,
those gentle twins I know so well.

You want it all to end,
but I am greedy
and I won't let you go,
crowding you
with my need till
we are both so tired.

Tonight,
you will lie down,
then I,
and we will wade together into sleep.
Already, I feel a thump
and shift as the day settles,
docking snug against the night.

Later,
there will be
the breathing we make—
the sighs and slow lament
between us in our bed,

ghost arguments
won,
lost.

Orchard

Three days of rain
and the Mirabelles drop into the grass,
sucked off their knob of branch
by the gravity of ripeness.

My dear, who knows he has
few harvests left
just shakes his head and smiles.

We live like the plum trees—
dumb on sun and sugar
until our lives fall.

Garden on Thanksgiving Morning

Pathways raked in July
are covered with leaves,
nothing thriving but billows of chickweed,
sturdy rosettes of hawksbeard and mahonia
which waves handfuls of yellow at the sky.
Brush dragged into piles now shelter quail
who butter the gloom with their soft chuffs,
and cause me to pause
before I pick the salad greens for lunch.

Last spring, a pheasant stood
where I stand now,
resting from the violence
of the season's mating ritual.

One June, two eagles,
fighting for primacy,
spiraled down from the blue,
almost strafing my back as I knelt below.

There was the afternoon a coyote
strolled through the garden,
stopping for a drink from the water bowl
next to our sleeping dog.

I recall these miracles
as the dull thrum of rain begins to build.

Our old chairs remain
where I placed them in warmer days,
claiming a picturesque view
of the Wapato wetland to the south.
I remember sitting together
in the fragile light of last Thanksgiving,

how we enjoyed the valley below,
tracing the longhand of the tree line,
its vertical green of Doug firs
balancing the em-dash
of our neighbor's metal roof—
how we never saw what was coming.

Pruning the Orchard

Early evening rolls down the mountain,
gathering in the firs above us—
the valley floor, anchored to the clay,
is locked in the inner chambers of spring.

Not ready myself to make the first cuts,
I follow you through the work.
We wade through pasture,
our boots hidden in the grass
which swells like surf in the breeze.

Our dogs are buried
somewhere below us,
their bones uncoupled by now,
floating among the roots.
Their ghosts roam around us,
still hunting for voles
while the orchard shivers,
a wild creature emaciated by winter—
tall whips wagging in the wind.

As if asking permission,
you pause and address each tree.
You approach, saw extended,
explaining as you cut—
branches falling around us,
a rusty treasure of sun and minerals.
We move deep into trembling crowns,
finding the weak and dying places,
freeing each tree
to float toward an easy June.

Our own ghosts are here too—
younger versions

striding through the meadow,
laying out the grid—
Mirabelle plum
and damson,
the prune d'Agen,
enough room for
Ashmede Kernel apple, Renette,
the Golden Gem,
Danube cherry, Montmorency,
Jubileum.

January Lonely

September's green coin spent long before
the turning of this cold day,
I watch a blade of sunlight
slide deep into the trees,
catching on the dry leaves
and lighting up the birds
who stayed through the winter.

If you were standing here at the window,
you could remind me of each bird's name—
the chipping sparrow's eye stripe
and the fox sparrow's crown,
and I would forget,
as I always do,
knowing you would explain again.

You promised to tell me
when the great horned owl
settles on her nest
in the snag above the back door
as she has for so many springs.
If you were here,
I would ask you to promise again.

But today is pounding on the door,
and I am caught
with our forty years in one hand,
and a plea for more time in the other.
My dear, I have such blankness
when I think about the future,
such wonder
at how we ever thought we could prepare.

A singer's voice on the radio
echoes through our rooms,
saying how much she loves me,
how we shall catch up some other day.
If I could ask,
you would have told me her name.

Winter Marriage

Cold wind works its way
inside my coat
as I wade through a wet field,
gathering mustard.
The leaves fight like fish flapping—
I pen them deep inside the bucket.

Voles have been busy,
scored the beets and cored each carrot's heart.
I imagine them snugged together
somewhere below my boots,
their fat pelts steaming in the dark—
I hope my stamp startles them awake.

A heron,
hunting for mice
on the long slope to the south,
opens her wings and lifts from the mud,
leaving me more alone as I hoist the harvest
with a huff and grumble of effort.

Several buckets to go,
depressed by the grey thumb of rain
slowing me down,
only some stubborn drive keeps me moving.
Glasses fogged,
I feel my way along as puddles spill into my boots.

Behind me trail forty-four years
since your question and my answer,
which despite this weather,
despite you as well,
working inside at your warm, dry desk,
would still, after all this time, be *yes*.

Walk with Me Through the Field

Trace the furrow
with your eye to the dark edge
just furring with green.

Listen as the wind rattles dry pods,
shaking out last year's seed—
the pasture is opening itself to Spring.

Harvest the young mustard
and bring in the dandelion greens.
After the lean time of winter,
this is what we need now—
the sharp tang of mending.

Stumbling through our span,
we drag our sorrows over the land,
expecting the land to forgive
and carry our wreckage down to its roots.

We bury our dead like treasure,
to blossom and fruit in the hand of God,
as if the only world is the world to come.
The earth takes it in
and takes us in as well.

Look down.
Your own story is here—
weeds made beautiful
by struggling up through rough ground.

Believe in this land—
even through rubble
living things ascend.

He Calls Me from the Road

Understand, we just spent
forty minutes loading the van with produce,
fighting about a job
we've done a thousand times

        and I'm still upset
        because his taste buds
        are wrecked from the chemo
        and we can't share basil anymore.

So, he calls me from the road,
with Vivaldi's *Summer Concerto in C*
fighting with the V8's struggle up Bald Peak,
to tell me he just saw a funny dog
and he wants me to laugh

        like I would have before—
        but he already hurts
        and it's not even nine.

Stop, I say, *come back and pick me up.*
Then, I climb in next to him
and we drive up Bald Peak
as the oaks above us
shake their fists in the wind
and Teresa Berganza bellows
at her barber of Seville
so loud that I just have to laugh

        and laugh till I cry.

Sometimes It's So Beautiful Here

I will miss
these long days in August
when a green fever shakes the earth
and Afternoon
unbuttons her blouse low enough
to flood the oaks in the canyon with light,
each leaf singing.

Gratitude and Acknowledgments

Much of the work in this book is the result of my long partnership with my husband, Anthony, and two decades living and working together on our farm. Thank you for so much, my dear.

It was my great good fortune that Linda Colwell convinced me to take writing more seriously. I owe so much to Kwame Dawes and Marvin Bell who helped shape and sharpen my poetry with their relentless challenges and fierce encouragement while I was working toward my Master's degree. I am grateful to be part of a community of poets who share their command of words and are generous with their time. My deep gratitude to Lana Hechtman Ayers for her skill and gentle guidance in turning a loose collection of work into this book. I am fortunate to have had the patient support and insightful editing assistance of our daughter, Caroline, a writer herself, who has her father's intelligence and her mother's stubbornness.

Thank you to *Windfall Journal* for publishing "Wild" and "Harvesting Chicory."

Thank you to the Oregon Poetry Association for selecting "Garden on Thanksgiving Morning" to share first place in the new poets category of the Spring 2021 contest.

Note: The poem "4 Glover Circle" Somerville paraphrases a line from Denise Levertov's "The Métier of Blossoming" from her collection *This Great Unknowing, Last Poems*. New Directions Press, 1999, p. 12.

About the Author

Caroline Boutard was born in Boston, Massachusetts, and spent her early life in New England. She spent many years working with plants at the botanic garden where she met her husband, Anthony, and while building gardens for others. She was Denise Levertov's gardener while they both lived in Somerville, Massachusetts, though most of what they discussed was the terrible state of Denise's backyard soil.

She lives in Gaston, Oregon, where she and Anthony run Ayers Creek Farm. Caroline holds a Master of Fine Arts in Poetry from Pacific University.

www.ingramcontent.com/pod-product-compliance
Lightning Source LLC
Chambersburg PA
CBHW022010120526
44592CB00034B/774